This ***Teine Pasifika Wellbeing Journal*** is designed to help you feel **SEEN**, **HEARD** and **VALUED** for the amazing and unique person you are. Culture, identity and wellbeing are interconnected. This is why it is important to strengthen and safeguard each of these areas in our lives to help us become the best version of ourselves.

*"Our power as Pasifika starts with fully stepping into our Pasifika light, which will always help guide and bring you back home to yourself."*

**Dahlia Malaeulu** | Author of Teine Sāmoa

# SEEN

**Being seen is more than how**
**we are viewed by others or**
**what the world sees on the outside.**
**It is when who we are and what**
**we are is fully understood and received.**
**We all deserve to be acknowledged,**
**recognised and seen in all the worlds**
**we live in but it all starts**
**with how we see ourselves.**

# WHAT DO YOU SEE?

When you look in the mirror, what do you see?

What experiences have shaped how you see yourself?

*How do you think the following groups see you and why?*

Family

Church

School

Work

Community or Society

# VISIBILITY: SOCIAL MEDIA

Social media is part of everyday life. It is used to message, share and stay up to date with news and events. But it is also important to be aware of the impact social media has on our mental health and wellbeing. Research has shown that social media has led to increased bullying, anxiety, depression and body image issues. This is why it is important to press pause and check in on your own social media usage from time to time.

Answer the following questions by placing a circle along the continuum lines.

Social media for me is more about:

| | | |
|---|---|---|
| connecting | ........................ | consuming |
| communicating | ........................ | comparing |
| posting for likes | ........................ | posting with good intentions |
| positive and supportive comments | ........................ | negative and mocking comments |
| entertainment, school, work, and I can happily live without it | ........................ | can sometimes lose sleep, and I cannot live without it |

Over the next week, commit to taking a break from social media. Each day look in the mirror and in a few words complete the following tasks:

**MONDAY:** Describe the person you see looking back at you.

---

**TUESDAY:** Describe the spirit of the person looking back at you.

---

**WEDNESDAY:** Describe the ancestors who are guiding and supporting the person looking back at you.

---

**THURSDAY:** Write down how you want to be seen in the real world and online.

---

**FRIDAY:** Identify and describe what needs to be done to achieve what you noted down from Thursday.

---

**SATURDAY:** Identify people who will be able to support and help the real you be seen.

---

**SUNDAY:** Write a thank you note to yourself.

# INVISIBILITY: FEELING NOT SEEN

Everyone can feel invisible at times and it's important to know and assess what can make you feel this way to help monitor and protect your mental health and wellbeing. Tick any of the following that apply to you:

I feel invisible when:

- ○ My ideas or opinions are ignored
- ○ I am automatically judged or discriminated against
- ○ My name is said incorrectly
- ○ I am not taken seriously
- ○ People don't know what I have been through
- ○ Hurtful or offensive jokes being made about myself, people I care about or Pasifika peoples
- ○ People don't understand what it is like to be Pasifika
- ○ People make assumptions about my life
- ○ I feel rejected or not included
- ○ My strengths and skills are overlooked
- ○ Other:

Why are Pacific Island names still being mispronounced?
Pacific peoples were always scientists, technologists, engineers, artists, and Mathematicians.
Report finds gender, ethnic disparities in NZ pay gap: Pacific women the hardest hit.
Pacific languages fade in New Zealand.
Pacific health report calls for urgent system change amid massive inequities.

Constantly feeling invisible can take a toll on our mental health and wellbeing long term. Also the answer to feeling invisible is not always doing or saying things to make you more visible all the time as each situation will require different approaches or responses. Here are some proven strategies to start with when you are feeling not seen:

### Strengthen your self-esteem:

Knowing, and accepting your strengths, your value and worth will help you to understand that regardless of how you are treated you are still important and matter. If one or some people, make you feel invisible remember that does not necessarily mean you are invisible to everyone else. Remember your people are those who see you, bring you up and cheer you on.

### Set clear boundaries:

Setting boundaries helps to remind yourself and others about what you will and won't allow. Healthy boundaries keep you and others safe from being hurt and help you to express yourself in a safe way before any harm is caused. Respecting and honouring your own and others boundaries are important for everyone, a good way to remember is to always respect and treat others how you would like to be treated.

**Clear communication:**
Being able to clearly state your thoughts and feelings is a skill that needs practise. Different situations call for different types of communication. It is important to practise advocating or speaking up for your personal needs, which helps to develop your voice. This is also why exploring your feelings and getting in touch with your emotions is important for everyone, and helps people to share them in safe and appropriate ways.

**Minimise or stop interacting with people who make you feel invisible:**
Some people are just not your people and that's okay. We all have a story and are dealing with things that the world cannot see, so sometimes regardless of our efforts people may not be in the right space to see you or hear your point of view. This is where it might be best to move on and protect our own mental health by choosing to surround yourself with people who see, hear and value you. The key is controlling what you can control, which includes how you respond to situations and who you surround yourself with.

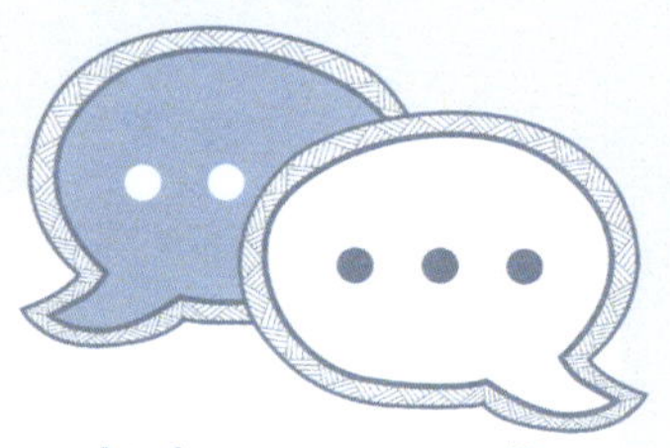

*Which strategy will you be working on?*

# PASIFIKA POWER

What are your Pasifika Superpowers?

- ○ Acting in love
- ○ Pasifika proud
- ○ Being respectful
- ○ Humble
- ○ Serving and supporting others
- ○ Leading others
- ○ Never giving up, being resilient
- ○ Critical thinker, analyses and plans
- ○ Resourceful
- ○ Developing orator, knowing when and how to speak in different situations
- ○ Creative
- ○ Courageous and brave

*What areas do I need to work on and why?*

# MY LEARNINGS

Press pause and think about the activities you have just completed in this section. What are the key learnings for you? Note them down or draw your learnings or add images or quotes in the space below.

*"Every day, I know that there is a student sitting in our fale, within our 'āiga who hasn't realised their full potential. This highlights the power of the life-giving words that we can speak each day to seek out the gold and support our students to fulfil their maximum potential."*

**Nila Uili** I contributing author of Teine Sāmoa

# HEARD

**We all have a voice and being heard**
**is more than being listened to.**
**When we are heard our feelings,**
**actions and intentions are validated,**
**acknowledged and understood.**
**This is why communication**
**is more than just talking**
**and listening to each other.**
**It also includes finding and**
**using your own voice.**

# YOUR VOICE: VALUES & BELIEFS

Your values and beliefs help guide your voice. Values are the principles or standards which you live your life by. Beliefs are usually learned from your experiences.

What are your core values?

What are some of your core beliefs about yourself? About your family, friends, school, work? Being Pasifika?

Whose voices do you hear and how have they impacted you? What are the messages you have received from the voices in these spaces:

Home

Church

School

Work

Community or Society

*"Maybe they thought I was mute, or at least treated me like one ... The thing was that I knew I had a voice. I rehearsed conversations in my head everyday - I just didn't know when to use it."*

**Vaia'ua'u Pilitati I** contributing author of Teine Sāmoa

# DIFFERENT TYPES OF COMMUNICATION

The four main types of communication are written, visual, verbal and nonverbal. As Pasifika we are raised to read and feel the energy within a room or from people before a word is spoken. It is important to remember that if we want to be heard we need to be able to understand the different ways we can communicate and receive communication:

**Verbal:**
Speaking, talking or using oral language to communicate

**Visual:**
Images that communicate or messages that can be seen

**Nonverbal:**
Messages communicated with no words usually via body language, facial expressions, body position or stance etc.

**Written:**
Conveying messages via the written word

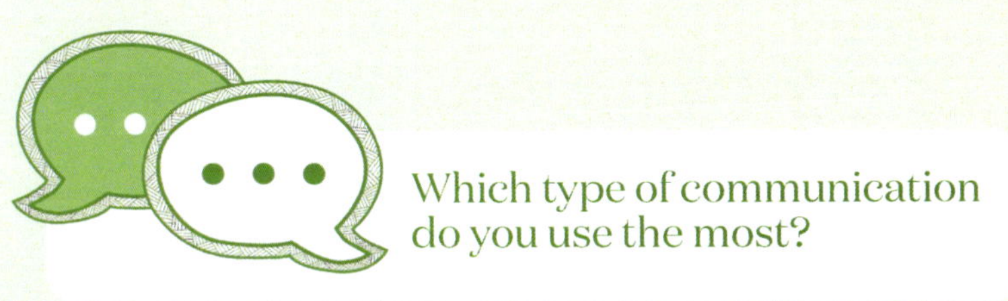

# IT'S NOT WHAT YOU SAY, IT'S HOW YOU SAY IT

When you speak, how do you come across to others?

Ask a friend or family member to describe how you come across to them when you speak to them.

How can the way you approach a conversation or communicate with others be improved?

# COURAGEOUS TALANOA

**Challenges are a part of life with many situations requiring some courageous talanoa. A courageous talanoa involves the following elements:**

**Timing** - Making sure everyone involved is ready to talk and is feeling safe.

**Authentically honest** - Sharing your experience by sticking to the facts and how the issue has impacted you.

**Listen** - Listening to understand not to react.

**Accountablility** - Accepting responsibility.

**Next steps** - Identifying what everyone will work on to make sure the issue does not happen again.

**Opportunities** - Confirming if there is a need for further support or future discussion.

**Action apologies** - Showing what sorry looks like through actions and following through on next steps.

Think about a courageous talanoa you have had and complete the following:

What was it about?

Was the issue resolved?

What helped?

What could you have done differently?

# MY TEAM

**It is important to surround ourselves with people who are there for us in the fun times AND the hard times.**

**Who are these people in your life?**

We become the people we surround ourselves with. Think about this statement and share your thoughts with someone.

Below is a list of some of the services available in Aotearoa that offer support, information and help for you, your parents, family and friends.

**1737 - Need to talk?**

Free call or text 1737 anytime, to talk to a trained counsellor.

**Youthline**

Call 0800 376 633 or free text 234 for 12-24 year olds.

**What's Up**

Call 0800 942 8787 or use the online chat at www.whatsup.co.nz for 5-18 year olds.

For more useful information and support visit **www.LeVa.co.nz**

# MY LEARNINGS

Press pause and think about the activities you have just completed in this section. What are the key learnings for you? Note them down or draw your learnings or add images or quotes in the space below.

***"I've learnt not to be afraid to speak up for my culture if I have to … How else will they know if we say nothing and keep allowing it all to happen? …"***

**Trinity Tauaneai** | contributing author of Teine Sāmoa

# VALUED

**Feeling valued reminds ourselves**
**and lets others know that we matter.**
**Research shows that when people are**
**valued they are more confident,**
**motivated and happy overall.**
**We all have value to add to the world**
**but it all starts with you valuing**
**who you are and what you are**
**before looking to others**
**and the world for validation.**

# VALUING ME

Finish the following sentences:

I am good at ....

I feel happy when I ...

I help and support others by ...

I love being Pasifika because ...

Something that I'm really proud of is ...

Something that makes me unique is ...

Something I am learning about myself is ...

Something I can do to make my world
a better place is ...

# SELF CARE

Self care can be difficult sometimes since it can be viewed as being self serving instead or serving others which is a major part of our Pasifika cultures.
But self care is essential in helping us to be the best versions of ourselves, which in turn helps us to be better for others. Complete the activity below.

What do you do to take care of yourself?

| PHYSICAL | MENTAL | SPIRITUAL |
|---|---|---|
| ○ Exercise | ○ Read | ○ Pray |
| ○ Sports | ○ Stay connected with others | ○ Go to Church |
| ○ Walk/Move | ○ Relax | ○ Sing |
| ○ Dance | ○ Alone time | ○ Dance |
| ○ Sing | ○ Time in Nature | ○ Writing |
| ○ Creative Activity | ○ Set goals | ○ Meditation |
| ○ Stay Hydrated | ○ Visualization | ○ Time in Nature |
| ○ Eat healthy foods | | ○ Quiet time |

**OTHER:**

# SELF TALK

Self talk is the way you talk to yourself, or your inner voice. Everyone has one. Think about what you sometimes or always say to yourself.
From the options below choose which ones you use or would like to start using:

- I am worthy
- I am enough
- I can do this
- I am open to learning
- I will grow from this
- I can bounce back
- I deserve this
- I know who I am
- I will be successful as who I am
- I am grateful
- I know what I am capable of
- I am creative and multi talented
- I am me
- I am needed
- I accept myself and others as they are
- I belong here

*"We have been studying the Dawn Raids this term, which I didn't even know about. He told us he wanted to learn more with us about our community and history and it helped me strengthen my understanding of who I am. And since it was taught to our whole class and assessed, it felt like it counted, that I counted, and that me and my history were important."*

**Angela Milovale** I contributing author of Teine Sāmoa

*"And just like the main character in my film says, 'It doesn't matter how much Samoan blood runs through your veins, or if you speak the language, or if you live on Samoan land, you are Samoan.' I tell myself this now and wherever I go."*

**Telesia Tanoai** I contributing author of Teine Sāmoa

# VALUING OTHERS

Making sure you are treating others how you want to be treated is important. How do you do this?

Think of someone in your life. Make a list of what you say or do to show them that they matter or are important to you. Alternatively, interview this person about what you do or say to make them feel valued:

# VALUING OTHERS

Our languages, cultures and identities play a major role in our mental health and wellbeing. This is why, taking the time to develop and strengthen your cultural connections has major benefits and positive outcomes overall.

Note down what you would like to learn or know more about your:

Language

Family Connections

Land & History

Customs & Traditions

# GRATITUDE

Being thankful each day for the good things in our lives helps us to always look at the bright side of things. Other reasons include:

- Helps us to be present.
- More positive and optimistic.
- Deal with challenges better.
- More resilient.
- Lifts mood.

- Boosts energy.

- Decreases stress and anxiety.
- Improves self esteem.

What are the top 3 things you are grateful for right now:

1. I am grateful for ...

   because ...

2. I am grateful for ...

   because ...

3. I am grateful for ...

   because ...

Share what you are grateful for with another person.

# MY LEARNINGS: KNOW YOUR WORTH

Knowing your worth means acknowledging, understanding and accepting who you are and everything that comes with this. Use the space below to create a vision board about who you are, who you stand for and why.

*"... we want you to really get to know the real us. Our names, our cultures, our history and our languages. Teach it or learn it with us. This will help us feel like we belong and we'll know that you value us and who we are."*

**Teuila Ekanesio** | character from Teine Sāmoa

# DEAR SIS...

Write a letter to your younger self. What are the things you would say to help encourage, uplift and heal from the experiences that you will go through?

Dear Sis,

# NEXT STEPS:

Look back in your wellbeing journal
and note your goals down for each section:

**SEEN** ... How do you want to be seen?

**HEARD** ... How will you feel heard?

**VALUED** ... How will you value yourself?

What action steps will you take to help you achieve these goals?

**STEPS TOWARDS BEING SEEN**

**STEPS TOWARDS BEING HEARD**

**STEPS TOWARDS BEING VALUED**

Complete the following journal entries to help you monitor your progress and assess your needs along your wellbeing journey.

# WEEK 1

What are the highlights? Your wins this week? Feelings? Any challenges? Help or support needed? New learnings?

### SEEN

### HEARD

### VALUED

## Noticings, Wonderings, Thoughts, Ideas, Breakthroughs ...

---

*"...Through work we prosper ... We journey together ... My strength is not due to me alone but due to the strength of many."*

**Niusila Faamanatu-Eteuati** I Contributing author of Teine Sāmoa

# WEEK 2

What are the highlights? Your wins this week? Feelings? Any challenges? Help or support needed? New learnings?

**SEEN**

**HEARD**

**VALUED**

## Noticings, Wonderings, Thoughts, Ideas, Breakthroughs ...

*"There is so much working against us in the pālagi world ...*
*I guess this is what makes it even more important for us teine*
*Sāmoa to know who we are, what we are, no matter where we are."*

**Rebecca Sa'u** | Contributing author of Teine Sāmoa

# WEEK 3

What are the highlights? Your wins this week? Feelings? Any challenges? Help or support needed? New learnings?

**SEEN**

**HEARD**

**VALUED**

# Noticings, Wonderings, Thoughts, Ideas, Breakthroughs ...

---

*"It is my duty to serve with reciprocity, respect, belonging, family, trust and compassion. I have been a professional observer all my life and I now know that it is a great skill and asset. But I've also found my voice and the power of it."*

**Vaia'ua'u Pilitati** I Contributing author of Teine Sāmoa

# WEEK 4

What are the highlights? Your wins this week? Feelings? Any challenges? Help or support needed? New learnings?

**SEEN**

**HEARD**

**VALUED**

## Noticings, Wonderings, Thoughts, Ideas, Breakthroughs ...

---

*"My reflection stares back at me, asking who am I meant to be? Yes, I'm Samoan but I'm also Kiwi at least that's what the world keeps telling me, as I grow up searching for my identity."*

**Tutoatasi Vailalo** I Contributing author of Teine Sāmoa

# WEEK 5

What are the highlights? Your wins this week? Feelings? Any challenges? Help or support needed? New learnings?

**SEEN**

**HEARD**

**VALUED**

## Noticings, Wonderings, Thoughts, Ideas, Breakthroughs ...

---

*"I remember a student smiled excitedly as she told me, 'I've never danced outside of my home and church before.' This is something I will never forget. This student was able to find a home, away from home through our pese, siva, language, the meanings and stories behind it all."*

**Makerita Feite Tago** | Contributing author of Teine Sāmoa

# WEEK 6

What are the highlights? Your wins this week? Feelings? Any challenges? Help or support needed? New learnings?

**SEEN**

**HEARD**

**VALUED**

## Noticings, Wonderings, Thoughts, Ideas, Breakthroughs ...

---

*"Tears began rolling down my face. For the connection to my culture I had been searching for all my life ...
For my own parents and 'āiga who had to assimilate into the New Zealand way of life by sacrificing our language and our culture - and for so many of our tamaiti today who are still searching for who they are as a result."*

**Eleanor McLeod** | Contributing author of Teine Sāmoa

# WEEK 7

What are the highlights? Your wins this week? Feelings? Any challenges? Help or support needed? New learnings?

**SEEN**

**HEARD**

**VALUED**

# Noticings, Wonderings, Thoughts, Ideas, Breakthroughs ...

*"... our silence does not mean that we do not and should not have a voice."*

**Vaia'ua'u Pilitati** | Contributing author of Teine Sāmoa

# WEEK 8

What are the highlights? Your wins this week? Feelings? Any challenges? Help or support needed? New learnings?

**SEEN**

**HEARD**

**VALUED**

## Noticings, Wonderings, Thoughts, Ideas, Breakthroughs ...

---

*"She saw how fear, guilt and shame were not good motivators for our tamaiti and knew that her goal was to help them feel valued and develop their self-worth ... something she realised and wished that someone had done for her when she was younger."*

**Sinapi Faafetai Taeao** | Contributing author of Teine Sāmoa

# WEEK 9

What are the highlights? Your wins this week? Feelings? Any challenges? Help or support needed? New learnings?

**SEEN**

**HEARD**

**VALUED**

# Noticings, Wonderings, Thoughts, Ideas, Breakthroughs ...

---

*It is also important that Pasifika teachers are not seen as the 'go-to' or 'one-stop shop' for everything that involves our Pasifika children and their families ...*
*how will other staff build connections and positive relationships with our Pasifika community, if I am the only one who is initiating and interacting with them?*

**Trisha Daniels-Sopoaga** | Contributing author of Teine Sāmoa

# WEEK 10

What are the highlights? Your wins this week? Feelings? Any challenges? Help or support needed? New learnings?

### SEEN

### HEARD

### VALUED

# Noticings, Wonderings, Thoughts, Ideas, Breakthroughs ...

---

*"I wouldn't just be a pass mark to some of them.
Instead, they would show they care by learning about me,
my world and my culture which is really important to me."*

**Akenese McCarthy** | Contributing author of Teine Sāmoa

# WEEK 11

What are the highlights? Your wins this week? Feelings? Any challenges? Help or support needed? New learnings?

**SEEN**

**HEARD**

**VALUED**

## Noticings, Wonderings, Thoughts, Ideas, Breakthroughs ...

---

*"When they belong and know that we believe in them,
it makes it so much easier for the students to believe in themselves."*

**Nila Uili** | Contributing author of Teine Sāmoa

# WEEK 12

What are the highlights? Your wins this week? Feelings? Any challenges? Help or support needed? New learnings?

**SEEN**

**HEARD**

**VALUED**

## Noticings, Wonderings, Thoughts, Ideas, Breakthroughs ...

---

*"I don't know the language, I want to come home.*
*But with my ancestors' courage, I need to come home.*
*I will voyage like they did. I am coming home -*
*To my culture, to my language, to my people,*
*I will learn all there is to know,*
*because I will not be waiting for the long return home."*

**Tutoatasi Vailalo** | Contributing author of Teine Sāmoa

# DEAR SIS,

Write a letter to the future you, what would you say to her knowing what you now know. *What would be some of things that you would be most proud of? What is she like and how has she inspired you? Who has this young woman become? How has she honoured herself, her family and other people in her life?*

Dear Sis,

Notes:

Notes:

Notes:

Notes:

Notes:

Notes:

Notes:

Notes:

**“When we feel seen, heard and valued for who we are and what we are, our tamaiti and we as Pasifika will be able to succeed as ourselves. This is the dream.”**

**Dahlia Malaeulu** I author of Teine Sāmoa